WORLDS OF THE PAST

THE GREEKS

Jacqueline Dineen

new
Discovery
B·O·O·K·S
New York

First New Discovery Books edition 1992

Originally published by
HEINEMANN CHILDREN'S REFERENCE
a division of Heinemann Educational Books Ltd
Halley Court, Jordan Hill, Oxford OX2 8EJ

OXFORD LONDON EDINBURGH
MELBOURNE SYDNEY AUCKLAND
MADRID ATHENS BOLOGNA
SINGAPORE IBADAN NAIROBI HARARE
GABORONE KINGSTON PORTSMOUTH NH (USA)

© Heinemann Educational Books Ltd 1991
First published 1991

Designed by Julian Holland Publishing Ltd
Color artwork by Martin Smillie
Picture research by Faith Perkins
Editorial planning by Jackie Gaff

New Discovery Books
Macmillan Publishing Company
866 Third Avenue
New York, NY 10022

Macmillan Publishing Company is part of the
Maxwell Communication Group of Companies.

Printed in Hong Kong

First Edition
10 9 8 7 6 5 4 3 2 1

Library of Congress Cataloging-in-Publication Data
Dineen, Jacqueline.
      The Greeks / Jacqueline Dineen.
          p.   cm. (Worlds of the Past.)
      Includes index.
      Summary: Surveys the civilization, history, and culture of
Ancient Greece, including information about government,
religion, and family life both at home and throughout the Greek
empire.
      ISBN 0-02-730650-X
      1. Greece — Civilization — To 146 B.C. — Juvenile literature.
[1. Greece — Civilization — To 146 B.C.] I. Title. II. Series.
DF77.D56   1992
938 — dc20   91 − 512

Photographic acknowledgments
The author and publishers wish to acknowledge, with
thanks, the following photographic sources:
a = above b = below c =center
Agora Excavations 1970, American School of Classical
Studies at Athens p40b; Ancient Art and Architecture
Collection pp7a and b, 11a and b, 16a, 17, 19b, 20a and b,
21c and b, 22, 27, 32a, 36, 37b, 46a and b, 56b; Bridgeman Art
Library pp9 and cover, 58; C M Dixon pp4a, 6, 8, 13a, 21b, 23,
31a, 32b, 45b, 50b and cover; Ekdotike Athenon pp19a, 24,
25a, 34a and title page, 49, 55a and b; Robert Harding
Photographic Library pp26, 38a, 43; Hirmer Fotoarchiv
p31b; Michael Holford pp4b, 10, 12, 13b, 15a and b, 28, 29,
33, 37a, 39, 41b, 44, 50a, 51, 59a and b; Kunsthistorisches
Museum, Vienna p56a; Mansell Collection pp14, 16b, 38b;
Metropolitan Museum of Art, New York, Purchase 1947,
Joseph Pulitzer Bequest p40a; National Bibliothek
Osterreichische p25b; Picturepoint p34b; Planet Earth
Pictures p45a (photograph Flip Schulke); Scala p41a.
The publishers have made every effort to trace the
copyright holders, but if they have inadvertently
overlooked any, they will be pleased to make the necessary
arrangement at the first opportunity.

Note to the reader
In this book there are some words in the text which are printed in **bold** type. This shows that the word is listed in
the glossary on page 62. The glossary gives a brief explanation of words which may be new to you.

Contents

Who were the Greeks?

The works of Greek thinkers, writers, and artists who lived a very long time ago are still admired today. Students study the Greeks' ideas about science and law. Builders copy the style of ancient Greek buildings. People enjoy the beauty of Greek poetry, statues, and painted pottery. The influence of the ancient Greeks has spread all over the world.

The first Greeks

People first lived in Greece about 8,000 years ago. They led a simple life, hunting and trying to grow enough food to live on. About 5,000 years later a very different way of life began on Crete, an island off the coast of Greece. There, people learned to build and paint and make beautiful objects. Their **civilization** is called Minoan, after Minos, their king. This was the beginning of the first civilization in Europe. The people on the island of Crete knew how to read and write, but their language was not Greek.

The first Greek-speaking people began to invade the Greek mainland from the north and east around 2000 B.C. They learned from the Minoans and built palaces at sites like Mycenae. The Mycenaean

△ The Greeks were the first to use elegant stone columns to support a roof. Many ruins like this temple have been found and preserved so that we can still look at Greek buildings.

◁ Greek craftsmen made beautiful jewelry using silver, gold, and precious stones thousands of years ago. Some of the styles are still copied today. Pictures on Greek vases show artists making bronze statues. Not many of these statues have survived. Over the years, people melted them down to use the metal to make new objects. We know what some Greek statues looked like because later artists made stone copies.

civilization lasted 400 years. It ended in 1200 B.C. when more invaders came to Greece. Wars brought poverty. For nearly 400 years people had no money for buildings or time to make works of art. This period is called the Dark Ages.

Life began to change around 800 B.C. at the start of the Archaic period. Villages grew into towns, protected by hilltop fortresses. The people in each town and the nearby countryside lived as a group or small community called a **city-state.** By the beginning of the Classical period in 500 B.C., Athens was one of the most important city-states. During the next 200 years the brilliant talents of the Greeks reached a peak. Then came the Hellenistic period, when Greek learning and ideas spread to many other countries around the Mediterranean Sea.

▽ The Greeks do not call their country "Greece" in their own language. Their word *Hellas* now means the country of Greece. To the ancient Greeks, Hellas meant all the places with a Greek way of life.

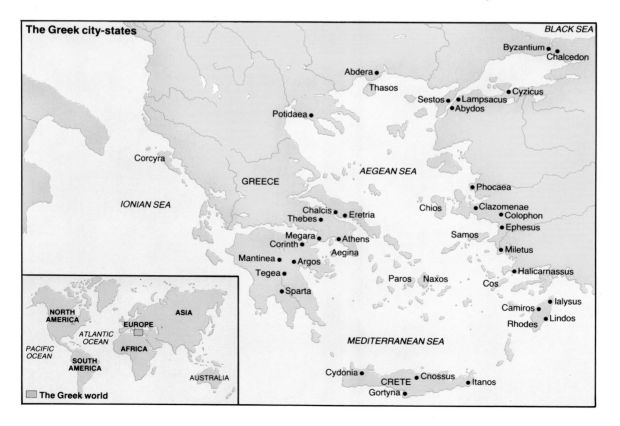

The Greek city-states

How we know about the Greeks

Visitors to museums today can see objects made and used by the Greeks. By looking at these objects, we know the Greeks used coins to pay for goods. Farmers used tools of bronze and, later, iron. Greek children played with toys made of clay. Such objects have been dug out of the ground.

People who study the buried remains of ancient times are called **archaeologists.** Archaeologists have discovered the ruins of whole cities buried deep in the earth. They can see how people built their houses. They also find everyday objects like bits of pots and jewelry. All these finds help to build up a picture of the past and the way people lived.

Archaeologists have to decide where to look. They study what is already known about the history of an

▽ Archaeologists at work slowly uncovering evidence from the past. Soil is carefully scraped away. Weapons and other metal articles may have to be cleaned. Sometimes broken objects are put together again so that we can see what they looked like. If pieces are missing, skilled workers may make new copies. Every find helps to complete the jigsaw that tells us about how people lived in the past.

◁ When Heinrich Schliemann found this gold cup at Mycenae, it was bent and squashed. Archaeologists have pushed the cup back into its proper shape. The poet Homer described a cup like this, with birds on the top of the handles, in the *Iliad*.

△ The picture in gold and silver on this bronze dagger shows men with shields and spears hunting lions. The dagger was found in Mycenae but the design is very like the work of Minoan artists. Archaeologists think artists from Crete came to work and teach in Mycenae.

area first. Sometimes they find clues in old books or maps. This was how the ruins of Mycenae were discovered. Mycenae was one of the hilltop **fortified** towns destroyed by invaders about 3,200 years ago. The ruins of the fortresses were gradually buried, but people still told stories about the Mycenaeans. About 400 years later, the Greek poet Homer wrote two long poems about the Mycenaeans. One poem, the *Iliad,* tells of a long war and siege at Troy, a city that was captured by the Greeks. The other poem, the *Odyssey,* describes the wanderings of the Mycenaean hero Odysseus after the war. Homer also wrote that Agamemnon, the commander of the Greek soldiers, lived at Mycenae. A German businessman, Heinrich Schliemann, loved the *Iliad* and the *Odyssey.* He decided to look for the lost cities. He found the ruins of Troy in 1870 and Mycenae in 1876.

Clues in words and pictures

Heinrich Schliemann decided where to look for Troy and Mycenae by reading Homer's poems. Although Homer is the first Greek writer we know about, archaeologists have found much older pieces of writing, but these are not books.

In 1900 Arthur Evans began digging at Cnossus, on the island of Crete. He found clay tablets with writing on them. There were two styles of writing but no one could read them. The two styles, or scripts, were called Linear A and Linear B. More tablets with

△ Mycenaeans inscribed the words on these clay tablets about 3,400 years ago. This script is called Linear B. The tablets are palace records of payments and lists of jobs and goods.

The Greek alphabet

Capital letter	Small letter	Name	Sound
A	α	alpha	a
B	β	beta	b
Γ	γ	gamma	g
Δ	δ	delta	d
E	ε	epsilon	e (as in *bed*)
Z	ζ	zeta	z
H	η	eta	e (as in *bay*)
Θ	θ	theta	th (as in *think*)
I	ι	iota	i
K	κ	kappa	k
Λ	λ	lambda	l
M	μ	mu	m
N	ν	nu	n
Ξ	ξ	xi	x
O	ο	omicron	o (as in *pot*)
Π	π	pi	p
P	ρ	rho	rh, r
Σ	σ ς	sigma	s
T	τ	tau	t
Y	υ	upsilon	u
Φ	φ	phi	ph
X	χ	chi	kh
Ψ	ψ	psi	ps
Ω	ω	omega	o (as in *dome*)

◁ Many letters in the alphabet we use today come from ancient Greek letters.

Linear B script were found in Greece in 1939. An English schoolboy, Michael Ventris, began studying Linear B. It took him over 10 years to work out the language. No one has yet learned to read the older Linear A, the language of the Minoans.

From 700 B.C. many official records were carved in stone. These tell us about Greek laws and how places were built. We can also learn a lot about Greek life from writers who lived after Homer. The thinker, or **philosopher,** Plato wrote about his own ideas and about his teacher, Socrates. The historian Herodotus tried to separate the facts of history from the stories people told. Many works by Greek writers have survived because their pupils wrote out copies. The original books and papers have now been lost. For hundreds of years new copies were made and passed on.

The Greeks painted pictures of their daily life on jars, cups, vases, and bowls. Many buildings were decorated with stone carvings. These **sculptures** and paintings show us what people looked like and what they wore.

During the last century many archaeologists took their finds out of Greece. They believed they were saving them for the future. These things are now on display in museums in places like London and Paris, Berlin and New York. Some people believe that such finds belong in Greece.

△ Many paintings on Greek pottery show scenes from the stories in Homer's poems. They also show special events, such as festivals and details of daily life. These paintings tell us as much as words. It is surprising how many things are the same as the way people live today. This vase shows farmers collecting olives. Two men use sticks to shake the fruit from the tree onto a sheet spread on the ground. A third man picks up the fruit. Olives are still picked in this way on some Greek farms today.

The Greek civilizations

3000 B.C.	The start of the Minoan civilization on Crete	1200–800 B.C.	The Dark Ages
1600 B.C.	The Mycenaean civilization begins on the Greek mainland	800–500 B.C.	The Archaic Period
		500–336 B.C.	The Classical Period
		336–146 B.C.	The Hellenistic Period
1200 B.C.	Dorian invaders destroy the Mycenaean civilization		

Government and society

Greece was not a united country. It was a collection of city-states. Each city-state, or *polis*, was independent. At first each state was ruled by a king with a council of rich landowners, or nobles. By the end of the Dark Ages, these landowners had as much power as the king. This type of rule by a group of nobles was called an **aristocracy.** Sometimes an aristocracy was overthrown by a tyrant. Tyrants were people who took power when they had no right to it. Nobles and tyrants ruled with no written laws.

There were frequent struggles to change the form of government. By the beginning of the Classical period, some city-states were ruled by an **oligarchy.** In an oligarchy, the government was controlled by a few rich **citizens.** Other people had no share of power.

Around 500 B.C., a new form of government was introduced in Athens. It was called *demokratia,* which means government by the people. The English word **democracy** comes from this Greek word.

In Greek democracies, all citizens had a say in how the city-state was run. They could vote for people to run the city. The Greeks did not include women and slaves as citizens, so they were not allowed to vote.

◁ The Acropolis in Athens. The word *acropolis* means "high city." The acropolis of a city was built as a fortress against invaders. It later became the place of worship, with a temple to the city's special god. The city and the countryside around it together formed a polis. This was an area with its own government.

◁ Once a year, members of the assembly had the chance to ostracize anyone they disapproved of. Each citizen who wanted to, scratched a name on a broken piece of pottery. All the pieces, called ostraka, were collected and counted. If there were more than 6,000 votes, the person with the most votes against him was exiled for ten years. Several ostraka have been found by archaeologists. One of these shows the name Aristides.

How democracy worked in Athens

Each Athenian citizen was a member of the assembly. The assembly met periodically and any citizen, rich or poor, could speak at these meetings. A council of 500 was chosen each year by drawing lots. The council decided what was to be discussed at the assemblies, and council members also looked after the management, or **administration,** of the city. A lottery was also used to choose a board of ten generals who were responsible for the protection of Athens against invaders.

Writers such as Plato, Thucydides and Aristotle provide information about Greek government. Aristotle wrote a long work, *Politics,* in which he discussed democracy and methods of government.

◁ Every year citizens of Athens took their turn to be judges, public officials, or council members. Using bronze voting disks, the judges gave their verdicts on quarrels between citizens. If the majority of disks had solid knobs, the person was judged innocent. However if the majority were hollow, the verdict was guilty.

Clothes and appearance

We know a great deal about Greek clothes and hairstyles from the literature of the time and from statues and paintings on pottery. The climate of Greece was dry, with mild winters and very hot summers. People kept cool by wearing loose and simple clothes. Men and women both wore a tunic called a **chiton.** Men wore short tunics for work and long ones for special occasions. These formal tunics often left the right shoulder bare. Women wore ankle-length chitons. In cool weather they wore a shawl, or **himation.**

Tunics and cloaks were kept in place by ornate brooches. Some women wore jewelry in their hair. Rich women dressed their hair around elaborate headdresses and bands. Fashions were always

◁ A man's formal robe was draped and fastened with a brooch. Sometimes the men wore a cloak over the robe.

changing, but women could buy wigs in the new styles from the market. Writers joked about the elaborate new hairstyles women had to wear. Men had fashionable hairstyles as well. In Athens, men visited the hairdresser as often as women, and both men and women wore perfume. Some women wore simple forms of **cosmetics,** such as chalk to whiten their faces or berry juice to redden their lips.

Most Greek clothes were made of wool. Some people bought cloth dyed in bright colors for their clothes. Wealthy women could buy lighter cloth called **linen.** Linen is made from the fine stems of a plant. Some clothes had patterns embroidered on them.

Only rich people in the cities could afford to buy all these luxuries. Most Greeks were poor farmers. They kept a few sheep and the women of the house dyed the wool and spun it into **yarn.** Then they wove it into cloth to make simple chitons and himations. Working men wore short brown tunics. Men and women went barefoot or wore leather sandals.

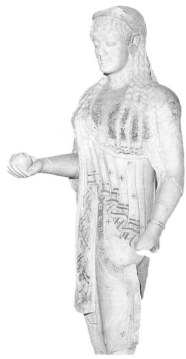

△ The chiton was a rectangle of material which was folded and fastened at the shoulders. This woman wears a himation over the chiton.

◁ All women except slaves wore their hair long. Some women let it fall in loose curls but most pinned or tied it into fashionable styles like the ones on this vase painting. They used wide ribbons or a hair net called a sakkos. By about 500 B.C. some Greek women were dyeing their hair. When they went out they wore a veil called a calyptra. This could be pulled down to hide the face or put on the head as protection against the sun.

Family life

Plutarch wrote about the lives of Greek leaders in his best-known books. The plays of Menander and Aristophanes describe the lives of ordinary people. Family life was important in Greece. People felt it was their duty to get married and have children. Marriages were arranged by the fathers of the couples. A husband and wife did not have to be fond of one another. A wife was chosen because she was suitable to be a mother. She was also expected to give money as a dowry to her husband. Sometimes the bride did not meet her new husband until the wedding **ceremony.**

Girls were normally married when they were about 15, but men were usually older. Plato thought that men should marry between the ages of 30 and 35. "It is a crime to refuse to take a wife," he wrote. Men over 35 years old who refused to get married could be fined or punished.

The wedding ceremony took place at home, not in a temple. The bride wore a white dress and a veil, like some brides today. On the wedding day, the

▽ Some Greek paintings show a chariot drawn by horses in the marriage procession. Only the richest families could afford a chariot. Most brides rode to their new home in a cart drawn by mules or oxen. The bride sat with her bridegroom, with his best friend behind. Friends followed on foot with presents.

bridegroom went to the bride's house with his friends. The bride's father announced to the bridegroom that he was giving his daughter to him. The girl then rode in a chariot or a cart with the man back to his house. He carried her across the **threshold** of the house. The bridegroom's family greeted the couple and led them to the hearth, where a fire burned. The fire was a symbol of family life. The couple knelt by the fire and prayers were said. The next day, the bride's family came with presents for a feast. The presents were usually painted bowls, cosmetics, boxes, and oil jars.

A woman's life

Once a woman was married, she spent most of her time at home. She only went out, with a maid, to shop in the market. Many wives had slaves and servants to work for them. In smaller houses, wives spent their time cooking and doing other household chores themselves.

A husband could divorce his wife at any time, but he had to give her back her dowry. She went home to her parents and the children stayed with the husband. Wives could divorce their husbands, but they had to give a reason in writing. A husband could also marry his wife off to someone else, without her agreement!

The naming of children

A new baby was named when it was ten days old. The Greeks did not have family names. A son was often named after his father or grandfather, and a girl after her grandmother. Some children were named after heroes or gods.

Relatives and friends were invited to the naming ceremony, or **amphidromia.** They brought small gifts and toys for the child.

△▽ Greek children played with hoops, balls, and kites. They had toys made of pottery. Archaeologists have found many examples, like whipping tops and this doll. This baby-feeder has a spout which would be covered with a nipple of cloth or leather.

Going to school

Children played at home until they were six or seven. Vase paintings and stone carvings show many scenes of mothers and children and of children playing with toys. Children were often cared for by a nurse. Sometimes the nurse remained with the family for many years. In Homer's poem the *Odyssey,* the nurse is the only person in the household who recognizes Odysseus when he returns after 20 years.

Most boys went to school when they were seven. They were taken by a slave called a pedagogue who made sure they behaved properly. Girls did not go to school. They learned at home and helped their mothers with household tasks. Some families could not afford to send their children to school. The children had to help with work on the farm.

Plato wrote in detail about education in Athens. Education was divided into three sections: letters, music, and athletics. These lessons are shown on many vase paintings. The boys learned to read, write,

△ Teachers taught pupils to read from texts written on scrolls of papyrus. This was a paperlike substance made from a tall, thin plant. Scrolls were long sheets of papyrus, rolled-up. The texts would be written in ink. The pupils read the work of the poets, mainly Homer. They had to learn long passages by heart. In this vase painting a girl is reading from a scroll.

◁ Greek children learned to write on soft wax. The stylus scratched letters into the wax-coated surface of the writing tablet. Afterward the wax could be smoothed over and the tablet was ready to use again. It is sometimes difficult to read Greek writing on pottery because words are spelled in different ways. The artists may have made mistakes because they were not taught well.

The Greek philosophers
Before the Classical period, civilizations had thought of brilliant inventions and made beautiful objects, but the people had simple beliefs. The Greek philosophers changed the way people thought because they questioned the traditional views of the world. They had firm ideas about the way people should think and behave, and they encouraged people to reason things out and to work out their own place in society. These men began the discussion and exchange of ideas which is the basis of learning today. The most famous philosopher was Socrates. His pupil Plato and Plato's pupil Aristotle left many writings about the philosophy of the Greeks. Plato and Aristotle both founded schools.

Socrates, 469-399 BC

and count. They wrote with a pointed stick, called a stylus, on tablets coated with wax. There were no desks, so the boys propped the tablets on their knees. They learned to count using the beads on an **abacus.**

Many vase paintings show music lessons. Both boys and girls learned to play stringed instruments and a type of flute. When boys were 14, they went to the *palaistra,* or wrestling school. There they were trained in wrestling, running, jumping, and throwing the javelin and the discus. A javelin is a light spear and a discus is a flat, round weight. This training was supposed to make boys strong enough to fight. Boys from wealthy families left the school when they were 18 and trained as soldiers for two years. Poor families only sent their sons to school for two years.

Many boys went to work with their fathers. Names on pieces of pottery show that four generations all worked in the same workshop. Xenophon describes how boys learned crafts as **apprentices.** Some young men continued to study with a philosopher. Aristophanes describes the school in Socrates' house in his play *Clouds.*

Plato, 427-347 BC

Aristotle, 384-322 BC

Living in Sparta

Life in Sparta was very different from life in the other city-states. Spartans disapproved of the thinkers and artists in other parts of Greece. In Sparta, the only important thing was to be a brave soldier.

Children became the property of the state as soon as they were born. All babies had to be shown to the leaders. If a baby was weak or ill, it was left to die. Children remained at home with their mothers until they were seven. Then the boys were sent to a boarding school. There they learned to obey orders without question. They learned to read and write, but training for war was more important. The boys were divided into groups. Each group had a chief, who taught the boys gymnastics. The boys were taught to accept hardship, hunger, and pain. They slept in uncomfortable rooms and were given little food.

△ This bronze statue shows a Spartan warrior of about 500 B.C. The warrior's hair is arranged neatly under his helmet. Herodotus wrote that Spartans combed their hair before battle so "that they might die with their heads tidy."

◁ The founders of Sparta were Dorians who came from the north. They built their city on the banks of the Eurotas River in southern Greece. The plain was surrounded by mountains that protected Sparta from other invaders.

Life after school

All male citizens became soldiers when they left school. They had to give all their time to the city-state. They could marry but could not live with their wives until they were 30. They could not own their homes and had no luxuries. All this training made them the best soldiers in Greece, but their lives were very harsh.

The history of Sparta explains why they led such a strict life. During the Dark Ages, warriors invaded an area called Laconia and fought the people who already lived there. These warriors set up an army camp, which became the city-state of Sparta.

They made the Laconian people work as slaves. The slaves were called Helots, from the name of their village, Helos. There were more Helots than Spartans. The Spartans became excellent soldiers because they were afraid that the Helots would revolt.

The Spartan government was an oligarchy. Only a few people could make important decisions. These were the 28 members of the Council of Elders. The Spartans elected two kings. One king led the army and the other was the chief priest.

△ Even girls were trained to fight. This statuette shows a Spartan girl. She was probably an athlete. Spartan women led very different lives from women in the rest of Greece. They learned to jump, run, wrestle and to throw the discus and the javelin. This training made them strong and muscular. The Spartans wanted strong mothers for their sons. Spartan girls wore short, sleeveless tunics. Other Greeks were shocked by these clothes. They thought women's clothes should cover more of their bodies.

The gods of Olympus

Religion was important to the Greeks and, like many of the ancient civilizations, they believed in many gods. Thales, the earliest Greek philosopher we know of, said, "All things are full of gods."

People had many different ideas about the gods. Homer describes gods who looked and behaved like humans. Hesiod wrote a history of the gods and explained how Zeus used thunder and lightning to conquer rival gods. Thunder and lightning were thought to be signs of Zeus's anger. The philosopher Xenophanes thought there was only one god, who was not at all like a human. Another philosopher, Protagoras, was not sure that the gods existed at all.

Greek children heard stories, or **myths,** about the gods before they went to school. The 12 most important gods were said to live on Mount Olympus in northeast Greece. Stories about Olympian gods and heroes such as Heracles were told for thousands of years.

△ Herodotus and other writers explain why Athens was named after the goddess Athena. She found a baby and looked after him. He later became a king. He started the worship of Athena in his city and gave the city its name. This silver coin made in Athens about 470 B.C. shows an owl, which was the symbol of Athena. The people of Athens believed their patron goddess would protect their city.

◁ Mount Olympus is the highest mountain in Greece, rising to 9,570 feet (2,917 m). The ancient Greeks thought of Mount Olympus as the home of the gods.

The twelve Olympian gods

Zeus: the chief of the gods. God of the sky, storms, thunder, and lightning. He married many goddesses, including Hera.

Hera: the wife of Zeus. Goddess of marriage and childbirth.

Poseidon: Zeus's brother and god of the sea. He used his trident to cause rough seas and earthquakes.

Demeter: goddess of farming and crops from the earth, especially grain. She was the sister of Zeus and Poseidon.

Apollo: the god of light, thought, poetry, and music. He was a son of Zeus and Leto. People thought Apollo could tell them about the future.

Artemis: Apollo's twin sister and the goddess of hunting and wild animals.

Ares: Zeus and Hera's son, the god of war.

Aphrodite: the goddess of love and beauty. No one knew who her parents were.

Hermes: the son of Zeus and Maia. He was the messenger of the gods who took the souls of dead people to the Underworld, a place with no sun in the center of the Earth.

Hephaestus: Zeus and Hera's crippled son. As the blacksmith god, he made thrones for all the gods and goddesses.

Athena: the goddess of wisdom and war. She protected cities and arts and crafts.

Hestia: the goddess of the hearth and the home. She was Zeus's eldest sister and hated quarrels. One day Zeus announced that his son **Dionysus,** the god of wine, must have a seat on Olympus. Hestia gave up her place so there would not be an unlucky 13 gods and goddesses.

Apollo, the god of music, holding a lyre.

Artemis, the goddess of hunting.

Athena, the goddess of war, with her helmet and spear.

Temples and shrines

The Greeks spoke to their gods with prayers, gifts, songs, and festivals. People prayed to the god who could help them most. Family houses had altars in the courtyard. Vase paintings show soldiers pouring wine from a bowl onto an altar or onto the ground before leaving home. They were asking the gods to keep them safe and for victory in battle. Plato said all wise men should pray every morning and night.

There were temples all over Greece for the many gods and goddesses. Each temple had a priest or priestess who performed special ceremonies. People did not worship inside the temple, so the temple had to look very grand from the outside. The temple was built as a home for the god. The image of the god was inside. People left gifts inside. Then they

△ People believed that the gods liked rich and sparkling gifts. This golden bowl is decorated with three circles of acorns and one row of beechnuts. There are bees between the acorns in the outer row.

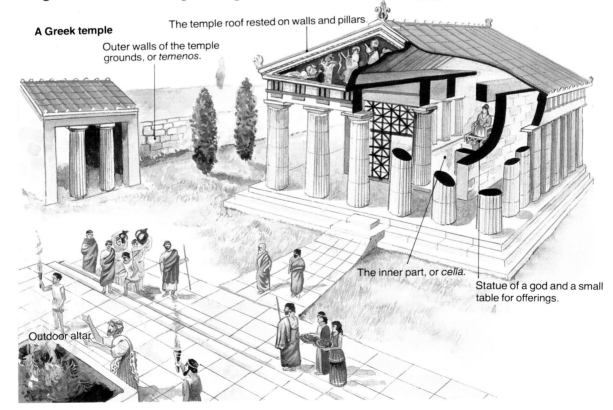

A Greek temple

The temple roof rested on walls and pillars.

Outer walls of the temple grounds, or *temenos*.

The inner part, or *cella*.

Statue of a god and a small table for offerings.

Outdoor altar.

◁ The first temple of Apollo at Delphi was wooden and burned down by accident. Aeschylus, Pindar and Euripides all described the splendid new stone temple, built just before 500 B.C. That building was damaged in 373 B.C. but rebuilt after a few years. The Greek travel writer Pausanias visited and wrote about Delphi 500 years later. Archaeologists began work 50 years ago. From the stones and from the descriptions of the ancient Greek writers they know what the temple once looked like. They have put back some pillars.

prayed at the altar in the open air. If they wanted a special favor, such as a good harvest, they killed an animal as an offering. They also made offerings if they thought the gods were angry. Each city had a special festival once a year. This was a ceremony for the god who protected the city.

If people wanted advice, they went to an **oracle.** An oracle was a priest or priestess who had special powers. People wrote their questions for the gods on lead tablets. The gods replied through the voice of the priest or priestess. The most famous oracle was at the Temple of Apollo at Delphi. King Croesus of Lydia went to Delphi and asked the oracle whether he should fight the Persians. The oracle replied that if he did, a great kingdom would be destroyed. Unfortunately for Croesus, this meant his own kingdom, and not that of the Persians!

Medicine and healing

When people were ill, they visited one of the temples of Asclepius, the god of healing. A story said that a snake taught Asclepius, son of Apollo, how to heal. The first doctors in Greece were the priests in these temples. The secret remedies they used to cure patients were passed down from father to son.

The treatments consisted of bathing, fasting, rest, and simple foods. People who were cured had their names and details of the cure carved on stone blocks in the temples. One of the most famous shrines to Asclepius is at Epidaurus. Many carvings about cures have been found there.

During the Classical period, a man called Hippocrates changed the Greeks' ideas about medicine. He did not rely on a god. Instead, he examined the patient himself to find out what was wrong and how the illness should be treated. Hippocrates founded a school of medicine on the Greek island of Cos, where he was born. Doctors had

◁ This stone relief was made as thanks for a cure. It shows what happened to the sick man. He went to the temple and made an offering to Asclepius. Then he slept in a room by the temple. On the right you can see Asclepius appearing to the patient in a dream and telling him how he should be cured. The snake leaning over the bed is the symbol of Asclepius. People thought that if the snake of Asclepius licked the eyes, it could cure blindness. In the morning, the patient repeated the dream to the priest, who then treated him. The snake is still the symbol of medicine today.

to take the **Hippocratic oath,** which listed their duties and how these should be carried out. Doctors still take this oath today. Hippocrates wrote about his work. Another doctor, Soranus, wrote a *Life of Hippocrates* about 500 years later.

About 100 years after Hippocrates, Herophilus founded a school of medicine in the Greek city of Alexandria. He was the first person to cut up human bodies and write about the insides. He taught doctors about **surgery.** Greek writing on stone tablets shows that doctors studied **herbalism** as well. One stone describes how an herb can cure soreness and scratches.

Patients could go to hospitals in Greek cities for free treatment. Xenophon writes of doctors who "from morning to evening go and see their patients." Patients had to pay doctors who visited them at home.

△ In this stone picture a man is offering a huge model of a leg as thanks for a cure to his leg. Archaeologists have found many models and stone pictures that have been offered by the ancient Greeks to their gods.

◁ A page from *De Materia Medica* of Dioskorides. He was a Greek doctor in the Roman army 2,000 years ago. This drawing was probably copied from real flowers. The book was bought in Constantinople 400 years ago and kept in a library in Vienna. That is how we can trace herbalism back to the ancient Greeks.

Farming the land

Farming in Greece is not easy. The Greek climate is hot and dry and the landscape is mountainous with thin soil. Between the mountains are small valleys with richer soil. The farmer has to choose crops that will grow best in these conditions.

In ancient Greece, farmers grew wheat, barley, fruit, and vegetables in the valleys. Herds of goats and sheep grazed on the dry mountainsides. The animals were kept for their skins, wool, and milk. Vines grew on **terraces,** which were cut like steps out of the hillside. Olives were the most valuable crop. Not only did the trees grow well in the poor soil but the oil obtained from their fruit was used for cooking and lighting. The trees also gave shade from the sun. Vase paintings show farmers at work and the crops they grew.

The farmer's life was not very secure. Hesiod tells us about the life of a small landowner in *Works and*

▽ The Greek farmer of today has the same problems as the farmer in ancient Greece. The countryside and the weather are still the same and the work on a small farm is not very different. Farmers keep donkeys, sheep, and goats. They grow vines on the terraced hillsides. They pick the grapes in August and make wine. Farmers in the valleys plant wheat and barley in the autumn. Crops are harvested in May. Greek farmers have always grown enough olives to sell to other countries.

When food was short in Athens in 591 B.C., the leader, Solon, made a law. Farmers could only sell their crops in Athens. The law did not include olives because the farmers grew so many.

The Greek months	
Gamelion	January-February
Anthesterion	February-March
Elaphebolion	March-April
Munychion	April-May
Thargelion	May-June
Skirophorion	June-July
Hecatombaion	July-August
Metageitnion	August-September
Boedromion	September-October
Ryanopsion	October-November
Maimacterion	November-December
Poseidaion	December-January

Days. He describes the farmer's year and his worries that the crops will fail. Landowners with small farms farmed the land themselves, with the help of slaves. If there was a bad harvest, the poorer farmers could not survive. They would become slaves. Some landowners were very rich. They employed **tenant farmers** to work the land. Xenophon describes an estate run by a rich landowner is his *Economica.*

◁ Scenes from everyday life were used to decorate walls and floors. This tiled floor shows a man plowing.

The Greek city

The old cities of ancient Greece were built over many years. Tiny streets twisted and turned, and buildings were cramped together. The Greeks of the Classical period loved order. When they could afford it, they rebuilt parts of their cities. Streets were laid out to make the pattern of a grid. The streets were straight and crossed each other at right angles. Buildings were arranged in neat, straight lines.

Wealthy citizens were proud to pay for new public buildings. Herodes Atticus gave money for a new theater in Athens. Most cities had a marketplace, or *agora,* in the center. Around the sides of the agora ran a covered arcade called a *stoa* where people could meet and talk protected from the sun and rain.

New cities were designed by town planners such as Hippodamus of Miletus. Aristotle wrote, "Hippodamus was a man who invented the planning

△ A stoa of the agora in Athens has been rebuilt. The American School in Athens began work on the site about 50 years ago. The houses that had been built over the ruins of the agora were knocked down. Nearly 5,000 people were moved to new homes before work could begin.

◁ Archaeologists have uncovered the city of Priene, on the west coast of Asia Minor. Priene is one of the finest examples of the grid system. The city was built on a hillside. At the top of the cliff stood the Acropolis. Below were temples and a theater for 5,000 people. The steepest city streets were built like stairways. There were blocks of four or six houses along the streets. In the center of the city were the agora and a stoa. There was a gymnasium where athletes could train and a stadium for athletic competitions lower down the hill. The city was surrounded by a strong wall.

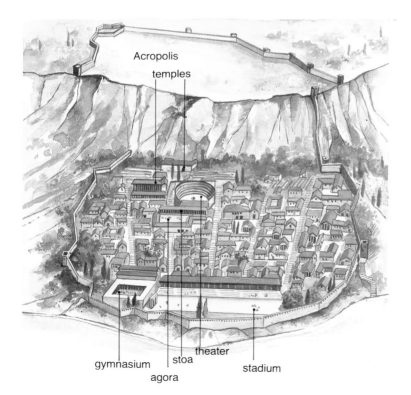

Acropolis

temples

gymnasium

stoa

agora

theater

stadium

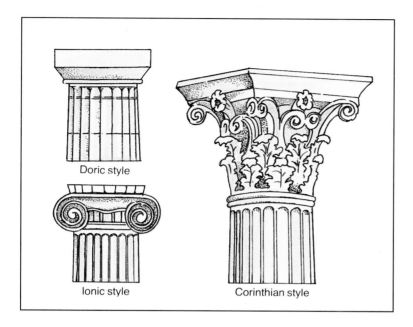

Doric style

Ionic style

Corinthian style

◁ The Greeks loved beauty. They used stone columns for most of their public buildings and temples. There were two main styles of architecture, the Doric and the Ionic. Doric columns, first used between 700 and 600 B.C. were thicker and stronger. They had a plain, square stone slab at the top. The Ionic style, used from about 600 B.C., was more graceful, with tall, slim columns. The top of the column, the capital, was decorated with carvings like a scroll. The Corinthian style developed from the Ionic style about 400 B.C. The capitals were larger and carved like the leaves of a plant called acanthus.

of towns in separate parts. He laid out the Piraeus with regular roads." Piraeus was the harbor area of Athens. It was built in 450 B.C. with straight streets on a grid system. The streets formed blocks for houses and separate blocks for public buildings.

◁ The Greeks began to use stone instead of wood for their public buildings after 700 B.C. Blocks of marble or limestone were cut from quarries. Then men carved the stone into shape. Columns were made by placing one piece of stone on top of another. They were held together by wooden pegs in the center of each piece. Clamps made of iron or bronze held stone walls together. We know from Greek writers that pulleys were used to lift the stones into place. We can see metal clamps and the holes for pegs in the ruins of Greek buildings.

A Greek home

The Greeks built their fine public buildings of stone and marble, but their homes were built of sun-dried mud bricks. These bricks were cheap to make and easy to build with, but they crumble after many years. House walls were built on a firm layer, or

▽ Archaeologists believe a comfortable house at Olynthus looked like this. Drains from the bathroom and kitchen led to the street. Most rooms had windows onto the cool inner courtyard. The windows did not have glass in them. The women's rooms were at the back. They sometimes had their own sitting room on an upper floor. There was a room for slaves. The dining room was for the men.

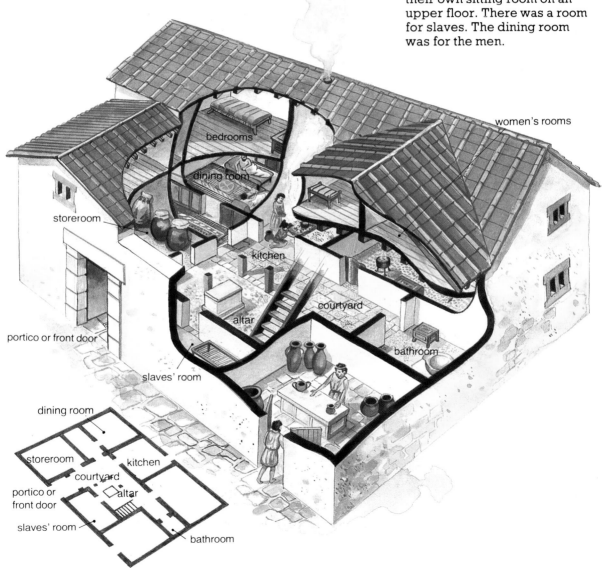

women's rooms

bedrooms

dining room

storeroom

kitchen

courtyard

altar

portico or front door

bathroom

slaves' room

dining room

storeroom

kitchen

courtyard

portico or front door

altar

slaves' room

bathroom

◁ This wall painting shows men at a feast. They are lying on couches and have low tables in front of them. In their hands they are holding their drinking bowls.

foundation, of stone, and larger houses had stone floors. In the cities, the stone from ruined houses was often reused for other buildings. About 100 houses of richer people have been found at Olynthus in northern Greece. People left the ruined city after a battle in 348 B.C. No one lived there again so the stones remained. Archaeologists from the American School of Classical Studies began digging at Olynthus in 1928. They found stone floors and items like pottery, bronze mirrors, and tools. These finds tell us what the houses looked like and what people did in the different rooms.

Furniture and decoration

Greek pictures show men lying on couches to eat. Dishes were put on low tables next to them. Because furniture was made of wood, it has not survived. Stone floors kept houses cool. There were no carpets. Some houses at Olynthus had patterned floors of pebble mosaics. Rooms were lit with small olive-oil lamps and heated with pans of hot charcoal. Some houses had a bath just big enough to sit in but most people poured water from a jug into a big bowl in order to wash.

△ From this clay plaque we know the Greeks kept clothes and blankets in chests. Other articles were hung on the wall. Behind this woman you can see her workbasket, a round mirror, an oil jug, and a cup. There is also a chair behind her.

Cooking and eating

In many households, the work in the kitchen was done by female slaves. They ground grain of wheat or barley to make flour. In parts of Greece today, women pound grain in the same way. This makes coarse flour for bread. Food was cooked over an open fire or in an oven made of pottery. Ovens could be carried outside. This kept the kitchen smoke free.

Rich city people could buy food. Farmers grew their own food and sold some to the cities. Farming families made bread and ate it with goat's cheese, eggs, and vegetables. Fig trees provided fruit. All the Greek city-states were near the sea. The Greeks ate a lot of fish, which they sometimes dried for use when bad weather made fishing impossible. Farmers did not have enough good land to keep animals for meat, so it was only eaten on special occasions or feast days. Families kept bees and sweetened their food with honey. They made wine and crushed olives for oil.

The main meal was in the evening. Men often had dinner parties to which their wives were not invited. A Roman, Cornelius Nepos, who visited Greece wrote that he found this very odd.

During the Classical period, people began to eat more complicated dishes. This food took longer to prepare and cook. Larger households had a cook. The character of a cook often appears in Greek plays of the time. Several cooks might be hired to prepare a big feast. These meals had four or five courses.

Music and entertainment

A feast was normally followed by some type of entertainment. Sometimes there was a **symposium** during which guests took turns speaking on a given subject. They often spoke against a background of music.

In a work called *The Banquet,* Xenophon

△ All the water needed by the household either for washing or cooking had to be collected from the fountain. This job was usually done by slaves.

△ Many pottery figures like this have been found in tombs. They may show the life of the dead person or they may have been toys. This woman is cooking over an open fire. She is using a fan to keep the fire at the right temperature.

describes a symposium that Socrates attended. There were musicians, a dancing-girl, and a jester. The girl turned somersaults through hoops fitted with swords. Plato's famous book *Symposium* records a talk given by Socrates.

The musicians played two kinds of stringed instruments. One was a type of lyre, the other was called a cithara. These were the most popular instruments. They also played a pair of pipes called an **aulos.** We know what these instruments look like from vase paintings. Also, an archaeologist found wooden auloi and bronze cymbals in Athens. Aristoxenus, a pupil of Aristotle, wrote about how to put musical notes on paper. Unfortunately, only a few fragments of written music have been found. We can only guess what Greek music sounded like.

◁ This painting on a wine jar dates from about 440 B.C. The woman in the center plays a type of harp. Above her is a cithara. On the left, another woman holds a pair of auloi. On the right, a young man holds a lyre. Writers of the time tell us that music was used in many ways in Classical Greece. Poetry was chanted to music. There were happy songs to celebrate events such as the birth of a child. Sad songs, or laments, told of a death. There were working songs and love songs. Dancing to music was a part of most Greek celebrations. As with the songs, there were dances for happy and sad occasions. Vase paintings show us the type of movements used in Greek dancing. They were full of rhythm and expression.

At the theater

Drama was a popular form of entertainment in Classical times. Every large city in Greece had a theater. Plays were performed on 10 days each year. People crowded into huge open-air theaters to watch. It cost two **obols** to get in, but poor people could get the money from the city-state. The best seats were kept for important citizens such as priests and judges. The audience stayed for the whole day and watched several plays. During the intervals, they ate the food they had brought with them.

Greek theater was different from modern theater because it was part of a religious festival. The earliest form of theater was a festival of songs and dances that was performed in Athens in honor of Dionysus, the god of wine. The songs were sung by a chorus. Speaking parts were introduced very gradually. At first, one or two actors stepped out of the chorus and spoke the main parts. This idea developed and by the Classical period, spoken plays were being performed. They were the first plays in the world. The plays were about the gods and heroes of legend so everyone knew the stories. They enjoyed seeing

△ The theaters were so large that the audience could not see actors' faces clearly. Stone figures show actors wearing huge masks. There was a sad one for a tragic character and a happy one for a comic character. The masks of tragedy and comedy are still the symbol of the theater today. There were also masks for men who were playing women's parts.

◁ The open-air theater at Epidaurus is still used every summer. The audience can sit on the same seats and see the same plays as Greek people did 2,300 years ago.

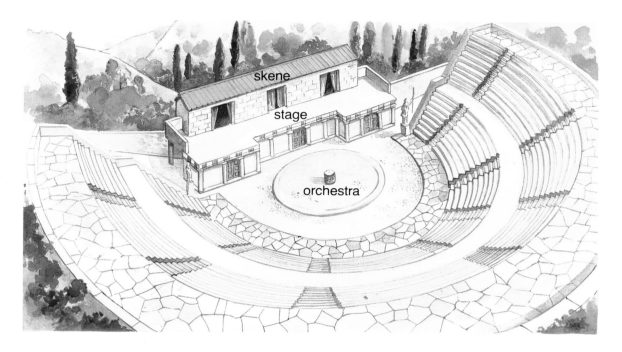

skene

stage

orchestra

how different writers told them. There were prizes for the best plays.

All the parts were played by men, because women were not allowed to act. There were only two or three actors in each play. They wore large masks to show what sort of character they were playing.

There were three types of plays. Tragedies were about solemn subjects. Comedies were about everyday things and made people laugh. A day at the theater usually consisted of three tragedies or three comedies, followed by a short play called a satire. This type of play made fun of a serious legend. The most famous writers of tragedy were Aeschylus, Sophocles, and Euripides. They wrote more than 300 plays, but only 33 survive today. The best-known comedy writer was Aristophanes, and we have 11 of his plays. People have admired the plays of these men ever since they were written and they are still studied and performed all over the world.

△ The architect Polycleitus designed the theater at Epidaurus about 350 B.C. Pausanias wrote that it was the finest theater in Greece. The theater is shaped like half a circle. There is room for 14,000 people. The stone seats are built into the hillside so everyone can see. The theater is designed so everyone can hear. The chorus danced and sang in the circular area called the *orchestra.* Behind that was the stage where the actors performed. At the back of the stage is the *skene.* This is a permanent background made of stone. Doors in the *skene* led to dressing rooms.

The games

Drama began as a way of honoring the gods. Athletic competitions began in the same way. Contests of strength were held at festivals for the gods. Gradually, they developed into organized "games." Competitions were held in running, jumping, throwing the discus and javelin, wrestling, riding, and chariot racing.

There were several different festivals. The Isthmian Games were held near Corinth in honor of the sea god Poseidon. The Pythian Games at Delphi were in honor of Apollo, and the Nemean Games at Nemea honored Zeus. The most famous of all were the Olympic Games held at Olympia in honor of Zeus. The Olympic Games were banned by the Christian emperor Theodosius in A.D. 394 because they were held to worship a Greek god. They were not held again until a French sportsman, Baron de Coubertin, organized the games at Athens in 1896. Since then, the Olympic Games have been held every four years in different countries. The events are based on the contests held by the Greeks.

Olympia was not the same place as Mount Olympus, where the gods were supposed to live. It was a **sanctuary** of Zeus in southern Greece.

▽ Archaeologists from the German Institute worked on the stadium at Olympia from 1958 to 1962. It is one *stade,* or 196 yards (180 m), long.

◁ Vase paintings show us different events. Athletes always competed naked. There were separate running, wrestling, and boxing competitions. The pentathlon consisted of five events: long jump, discus, javelin, running, and wrestling. For the long jump, athletes held weights made of stone or metal. They jumped from a mound, swinging the weights that helped to carry them long distances. Some of these weights have survived. The picture on this vase shows a young man with jumping weights, or *halteres*.

Archaeologists have uncovered the ruins of Olympia, so we know exactly what it looked like.

The games took place every four years from 776 B.C. They were held in June or July and lasted for five days. The date was announced by messengers who set out from Olympia and traveled all over Greece. The games began with a sacrifice to Zeus.

People came from all over Greece to watch or compete in the games. The athletes were not professionals but Greek men and boys who were very fit. Every city had a gymnasium where male citizens practiced every day. Any men except slaves and foreigners could compete in the games. There were even events for children. Women were not allowed to take part. The winners received simple garlands of olive leaves. Their prize was simply the glory of winning. To win at Olympia meant lifelong fame for the athlete.

△ Chariot racing was a popular event for the spectators. Vase paintings and statues show us riders racing their horses at great speed. The main event of the Olympic Games was the chariot race. Chariots were drawn by four horses. Later, chariots drawn by two horses were introduced. Prizes went to the owners of the racehorses or the chariots, not to the drivers.

Craftsmen and slaves

Most Greeks worked as farmers but in the cities some people had other jobs. Greeks did not like to work for masters. They preferred to be self-employed because it made them more independent. Craftsmen set up their own small workshops to make the things townspeople needed. The council paid self-employed builders and craftsmen for their work on new public buildings.

Some Greeks had workshops in their houses where they made their own pottery. Other people bought from craftsmen. Every household needed pottery plates, bowls, cups, and jars. Some children's toys were made of pottery. Craftsmen also made flat oil lamps from clay or metal.

Pottery for everyday use was often painted. Some artists wrote their names on their work. A potter called Euphronios had a large workshop in Athens. He made vases and at first he painted them himself. Later, the names of ten different painters appeared on Euphronios's pots. Sometimes two artists worked on one painting. Some of these paintings show us other craftsmen at work and the tools they used.

There were carpenters who made wooden

◁△ Cobblers made sandals and a type of boot with a pointed toe that men sometimes wore. In the picture on the left, a customer stands ready for the cobbler to draw around her feet so he can get the right shape for her sandals. In the picture above, the cobbler makes the sandal. Tools for shaping and sewing the shoes hang ready for use. Cobblers also used nails for the soles. Archaeologists discovered nails when they uncovered a shoe shop near the agora in Athens.

furniture and smiths who used metals such as iron and bronze to make plows, knives, and armor. The smith's warm shop was a popular meeting place in winter. Basketmakers used reeds or willow to make baskets that were used for storing wool or as containers for fruit or grain. All these workers were men. Women only worked in the home. Fathers passed their skills to their sons.

Some Greeks did not have to work at all because they owned slaves. Slaves were usually foreigners. They were often people who had been captured during a war and brought back to Greece. Rich families had many slaves and even the poorer farmers had slaves to help them. Slaves had no freedom. They were expected to do everything in the house. This gave Greek men the time to go to the assembly meetings and take part in the government of the city-state.

◁ Vase paintings show metalworkers heating metals in a furnace. Metalworkers made some household utensils such as knives and cooking pots. Ornaments such as buckles and military equipment such as helmets were often made in bronze. Jewelry was made in silver or gold. Sometimes precious or semiprecious stones were included. Archaeologists have found earrings, bracelets, necklaces, and rings.

The agora

To buy a pot or a basket, a Greek could go to the craftsman's workshop or to the agora. The agora was a large open space in the center of most Greek cities. Around the agora there were temples, law courts, and buildings where the assembly met. The word *agora* meant a meeting or assembly before it became a marketplace as well. Some cities also had market buildings. In Athens there was a corn exchange, where merchants bought and sold grain. The city of Megara had a building where perfume was sold. Archaeologists have found many perfume bottles there made of pottery.

The agora was divided into areas for different types of produce. They were all named "cheese," "wine," "fish," and so on. The goods were laid out on stalls. Some sellers had small covered shops with roofs and walls of reeds.

Potters, bronze workers, and stone carvers had workshops on two sides of the agora in Athens. The craftsmen got plenty of customers because the market was busy. At the edge of the agora, groups of slaves waited to be hired for work or bought by new owners.

△ These men are using balance scales to weigh goods. Greek weights were called talents. One talent was nearly 58 pounds (26 kg). The historian Herodotus wrote that King Pheidon of Argos introduced a system of weights and measures to Greece about 650 B.C.

◁ Archaeologists can often piece together enough information from ruins and the objects they find for artists to make detailed pictures of what a place may have looked like. This is what the agora in Athens may have looked like in Classical times. Pausanias wrote a detailed description when he visited the agora.

The bankers sat at counters on the agora, ready to lend money to people who needed it. They charged **interest** on the loan, just as banks do today. Each city-state had its own coins. Merchants often brought back coins from other city-states they had been visiting. They could change these coins into their own currency at the bankers' stalls.

Rich women only went to the agora if they wanted to buy something for themselves like perfume or jewelry. They did not shop for food or household goods. They did not even send a maid. The husband or his slave did the shopping. He chose the goods he wanted and then asked for them to be brought to his home. People did not have shopping bags. In his play *Lysistrata*, Aristophanes describes soldiers buying vegetable puree and carrying it in their helmets.

△ The fish seller on this vase uses a large knife to cut pieces of fish for a customer. The fish stall was an important part of the agora. In the towns people bought fresh food every day.

Greek coins

At first, the Greeks traded by exchanging goods. They did not use money until 900 B.C. Then they began to use thin rods of iron, called *obelos*. A handful or bundle of obelos was called a *drachma.* Coins were introduced about 650 B.C. Each city-state had its own design. Many coins have been found and some of the pictures on them show us what the Greeks thought the gods looked like. This coin from Dodona shows Zeus. Some tell us more about the city. The coin of Mende shows Dionysus on one side and a vine on the other. Mende was famous for its wine. In Classical times there were two units of money, the obol and the drachma. Six obols were worth one drachma. There was very little gold in Greece. Most Greek coins were made of silver.

Colonization and trade

Archaeologists have found Greek coins and articles such as pottery in countries outside Greece. This evidence shows us that the Greeks traded with other countries. The Greeks also settled in other lands and built cities with buildings just like those in their homeland. The ruins of these buildings show us where the Greeks settled. These places were called **colonies.**

Between 800 and 700 B.C., the population of Greece grew so fast that there was not enough land to grow food for everyone. The city-states sent people to find other land to farm. These people settled on land near the sea. They planted grain and vegetables to grow enough food for their own needs. Then they built new city-states. They had to be independent. They could not rely on help from the city-states they had left. As

▽ The Greeks founded colonies in Italy, Sicily, North Africa, and Asia Minor. The map shows these colonies and the goods they traded. Few trees grow in southern Greece or on the Greek islands. The city-states bought timber for shipbuilding from Macedonia to the north of Greece and from Sicily. Metalworkers needed tin from Britain and copper from Cyprus and northern Italy to make bronze. Most of the grain from Egypt and Sicily went to Athens.

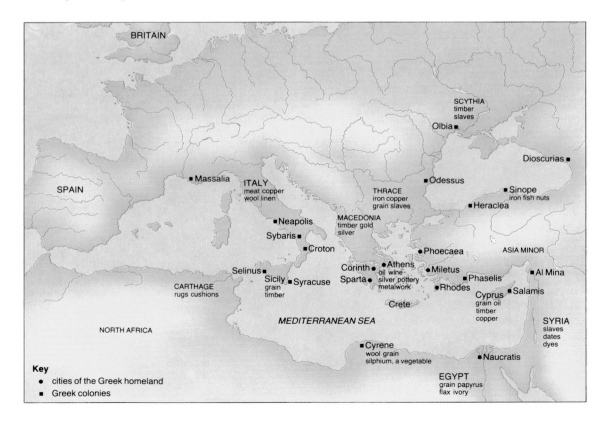

BRITAIN

SCYTHIA
timber
slaves

Olbia ■

Dioscurias ■

SPAIN

■ Massalia

ITALY
meat copper
wool linen

THRACE
iron copper
grain slaves

■ Odessus

■ Sinope
iron fish nuts

■ Heraclea

■ Neapolis

MACEDONIA
timber gold
silver

Sybaris ■

■ Croton

● Phoecaea

ASIA MINOR

Selinus ■

Corinth ●   ●Athens
            oil wine

● Miletus

■ Al Mina

Sparta ●   silver pottery
           metalwork

■ Phaselis

CARTHAGE
rugs cushions

Sicily   ■ Syracuse
grain
timber

● Rhodes

Cyprus ■
grain oil
timber
copper

■ Salamis

Crete

SYRIA
slaves
dates
dyes

NORTH AFRICA

MEDITERRANEAN SEA

■ Cyrene
wool grain
silphium, a vegetable

■ Naucratis

Key
● cities of the Greek homeland
■ Greek colonies

EGYPT
grain papyrus
flax ivory

the colonies became more organized, the people began to trade. They sent anything they had a lot of, such as grain, timber, and metals, to other Greek cities. They bought goods they needed, such as pottery, oil, and silver from Athens, or wool and papyrus from North Africa.

The trading fleets

Businessmen, or traders, organized the movement of goods between the colonies and Greece. They also traded with other countries around the Mediterranean Sea, like Syria, Egypt, and northern Italy.

Athens had a large fleet of merchant, or trading, ships. The ships were not owned by a big company. Each trader had his own ship, which he sailed from April to September, buying and selling at different ports. From October to March the weather was bad and the seas too rough to sail. Many of the traders were foreigners who were not allowed to own land in Greece. They **invested** their money in goods to export. Sometimes groups of men shared their money in order to buy goods.

◁ The land on the Greek mainland and islands was not good for farming and there was not enough food for everyone. Greek painting, sculpture, and architecture spread to other countries when Greeks traveled to found colonies. Ships carried goods and people between the islands, the mainland, and other countries. The quickest way to travel was by sea.

Transport

Greece has a long coastline. The easiest way to travel was by ship, so most people lived near the sea. Ships kept close to land whenever possible. Greek sailors did not like to sail across open sea. When they had to, they steered by the sun or by watching the stars at night.

Many large pottery jars, called *amphorae,* have been found on wrecked Greek ships. These sealed jars were used to carry oil, grain, and wine. They are evidence of the trade by sea between Greek cities. Merchant ships were big, wooden sailing ships. There was plenty of room for cargo, but the ships were slow. If the wind dropped, they could not move at all.

The merchant ships were often protected from pirates by warships called **triremes.** A trireme had oars as well as sails. It did not have to rely on the wind and could travel much faster than a merchant ship.

△ Greek paintings help archaeologists piece together parts of wrecked ships. This cup was made in Athens in about 500 B.C. It shows a heavy, wide merchant ship on the left and a long, narrow trireme on the right. Triremes were built for speed. They were about 114 feet (35 m) long and 16 feet (5 m) wide.

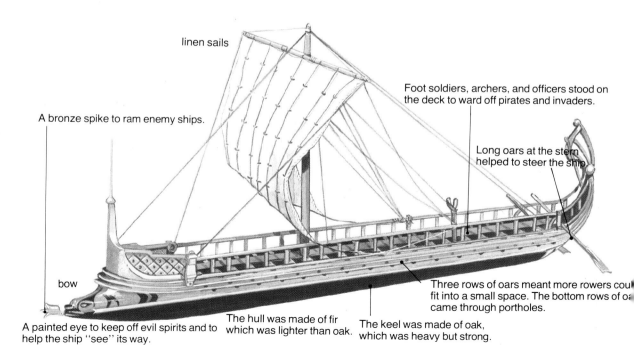

linen sails

A bronze spike to ram enemy ships.

Foot soldiers, archers, and officers stood on the deck to ward off pirates and invaders.

Long oars at the stern helped to steer the ship.

bow

Three rows of oars meant more rowers could fit into a small space. The bottom rows of oars came through portholes.

A painted eye to keep off evil spirits and to help the ship "see" its way.

The hull was made of fir which was lighter than oak.

The keel was made of oak, which was heavy but strong.

◁ Archaeologists work underwater as well as on land. They dive down to examine shipwrecks on the seabed. They make notes and drawings and check whether the ship can be moved. As Greek ships were made of wood, they rotted in seawater. Sometimes pieces are found and brought to the surface, where the wood is treated with preservative to keep it from crumbling. Often other things are found, such as cargo, or utensils and weapons. This is another important way of finding out how people lived in the past.

Ships may sink because of storms or during battles. Underwater archaeologists study historical records to work out where ships have been lost. In the 1950s, a sunken ship was located off Artemisium in Greece. The jockey in the picture was found in the wreckage. Years later more bronze pieces were found in the wreck by another diver. When the pieces were fitted together, the archaeologists found that they formed the rider's horse. So the horse and rider were reunited after 2,200 years.

If people traveled by land, they walked, or rode on horseback. There were also two-wheeled chariots and carts, and larger four-wheeled carts for carrying several passengers and luggage. Cargo was also carried by cart or in baskets on a donkey's back. There were no paved roads except to famous shrines, like those around Athens and from Olympia to the seacoast. The risk of being robbed or killed by bandits made land travel even more unpopular.

Greek soldiers

Each city-state had its own army during the Classical period. Sparta had an army of full-time soldiers, but in the other city-states young men trained as soldiers for two years when they left school. In Athens, they became the *ephebes,* which was a military training group organized by the city-state. They were sent to country fortresses or camps on the coast. They guarded the borders of the city-state of Athens from invaders and learned to be soldiers at the same time.

After this training, men were called up to join the army if there was a war. The main force of the army were the foot soldiers, or hoplites. Hoplites had to buy their own helmets, swords, shields, breastplates, spears, and leg protectors called greaves. People who could not afford this equipment became oarsmen on the triremes.

The hoplites fought in a **phalanx.** A phalanx was a square formation made up of 256 hoplites. Each soldier stood very close to the next man so that his body was partly protected by his neighbor's shield.

△ The Greeks had several styles of helmets. They were designed in different regions of Greece. One of the most successful was the Corinthian helmet like the example in the picture. The design did not change much for 300 years. This type of helmet protected the nose and cheeks as well as the head. Vase paintings often show plumes on Greek helmets.

◁ The painting on this bowl from the fifth century B.C. shows a hoplite in armor. He wears a short pleated tunic and a helmet. He carries a shield and a spear.

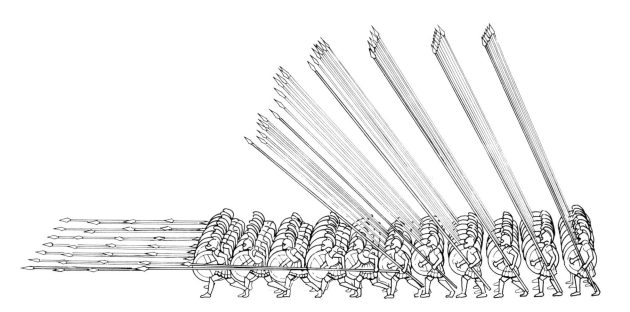

Peltasts armed with shields and spears were grouped on each side of the phalanx. Some armies had **cavalry** who rode on the outside of the whole group.

Phalanx fighting was very effective. First the peltasts threw spears at the enemy, then moved back behind the phalanx. The phalanx moved forward and forced the enemy soldiers to move apart. Hand-to-hand fighting followed while the peltasts and cavalry moved in on each side of the enemy and forced them to run away or be taken prisoner.

△ The long spears were an important part of the phalanx in action. The first five rows of hoplites held their spears out in front of them. They did not have to get too close to the enemy before striking them. Row after row of hoplites marched toward enemy soldiers, like a battering ram. If any enemy remained, the hoplites fought them with swords.

Greek armor

A good deal is known about Greek armor because metal lasts a long time and many examples have been found. The hoplite wore a bronze helmet and breastplate over a short tunic. He carried a bronze shield called a hopla. His legs were protected by shin guards or greaves that were also made of bronze. His weapons were a sword which was 27 inches (70 cm) long and a spear which was usually 6½ to 9 feet (2 to 3 m) long. The Theban army used spears which were 20 feet (6 m) long.

War on land and at sea

City-states such as Athens and Sparta were great rivals and often fought each other. However, when a foreign army threatened Greece, the city-states could ask each other for help.

To the east of the Greek city-states, the vast Persian empire had become very powerful under King Darius. In 499 B.C. the Ionian city-states rebelled against Persian rule, and Athens sent 20 ships of soldiers to help them. At first the Greeks were successful and they burned the important city of Sardis. After the Athenian soldiers had gone home, the Ionian Greeks continued fighting until they were defeated in 493 B.C. However, Darius wanted his revenge on the Athenians. In 490 B.C. he sent an army to attack Athens. The Athenian army, led by General Miltiades, managed to defeat the strong Persian force at the Battle of Marathon. Afterward an athlete called Pheidippides ran from Marathon to Athens with the

▽ Cyrus the Great made Persia the biggest empire in the world. When he defeated King Croesus of Lydia in 546 B.C., the Greek city-states in western Asia Minor became part of the Persian empire. Although each city-state had its own ruler, the king of Persia ruled over his empire from his palaces at Babylon, Persepolis, and Susa. The Persians were not harsh rulers, but the Greeks were independent people and they wanted their freedom.

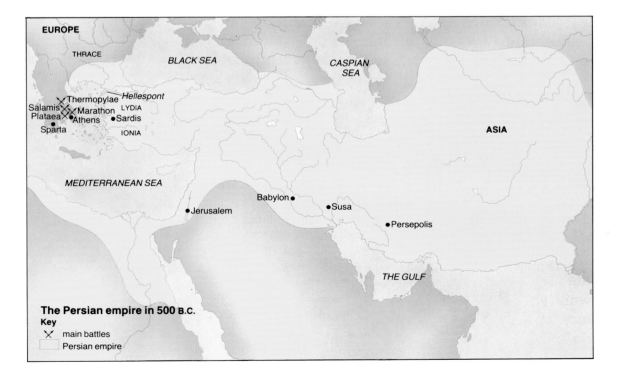

The Persian empire in 500 B.C.

Key
✕ main battles
☐ Persian empire

news. Marathon is about 25 miles (40 km) from Athens. This is the distance of marathon races that people run today.

Darius was furious at this defeat but he died before he could plan another war against the Greeks. His son, Xérxes, was determined to defeat the Greeks. The Athenian commander, Themistocles, persuaded the Greeks that they would only be safe from the Persians if they could defeat them at sea. The council agreed to spend the money to build a fleet of 200 triremes at Piraeus.

In 480 B.C., after ten years' training, Xérxes led his huge army into Greece. First they had to cross the Hellespont, the channel of water which divided Europe from Asia. In order to do this, the Persians tied 300 boats together to make a bridge.

The Spartans joined the war to help the Athenians, but their army was too small. Although the Greeks fought bravely, they were defeated at Thermopylae and the Persians marched on toward Athens.

△ After the Persian wars, the Athenians thought that Themistocles was too powerful and he was banished from Athens. This bust may be a true portrait of Themistocles. It was made by a Roman artist but he copied it from a Greek sculpture that no longer exists. The Greek original probably dated from about 460 B.C.

The battle of Salamis

Themistocles ordered everyone to leave Athens. The women and children went to the safety of the islands. The men joined the triremes to fight at sea. Themistocles planned to lure the Persian fleet to a narrow channel between the Greek mainland and the island of Salamis, where it would be difficult for the Persians to move their ships.

The plan worked after Themistocles had sent a false message to Xérxes saying that the Greek fleet was trying to escape. Xérxes sent warships to block the Greek escape. The lighter Greek triremes were waiting to attack them. In the battle the Persians lost most of their ships and the Persian army was finally defeated on land at the Battle of Plataea in 479 B.C.

The Athenian empire

Although the Spartan army had defeated the Persians at the Battle of Plataea, it was the Athenians who grew in wealth and power afterward.

The triremes Themistocles had originally needed before the Battle of Salamis had been paid for using silver from a mine at Laurion. The Laurion mountains were within the borders of the Athenian city-state. After their success at Salamis, the Athenians made their navy even larger. So although the Spartans still had the best army, the Athenians had the best navy.

However, the Greeks were still afraid of attacks by the Persians. The Athenians put forward the idea that the city-states should join together in a **league.** More than 200 city-states and islands joined. It was called the Delian League because its headquarters was on the island of Delos.

Each member of the league gave ships or money to build them. Using the ships contributed by the

△ Pericles was leader of Athens for 30 years, from 460 B.C. He planned magnificent new buildings to make Athens the most beautiful city in the world. He said he wanted his city to be "an education to Greece."

◁ The buildings on the Acropolis in Athens had been destroyed by the Persians. The Parthenon was built as thanks to the gods for saving the people of Athens. An architect called Ictinus drew the plans for the temple to Athena.

The Parthenon
A 40-foot (12-m)-high statue of Athena in gold and ivory was designed by the sculptor Phidias for the interior of the Parthenon. Over 500 painted statues stood around the temple. The carvings in the picture are part of the marble frieze that decorated the outside of the temple.

league, the Athenian navy was able to destroy a new Persian fleet in 486 B.C. The Athenian navy protected the other city-states and made them pay for this protection. Athens became more and more powerful. In 453 B.C. the Athenians moved the league's money to a treasury in Athens. They made all league members use Athenian coins. The league became an Athenian empire.

The people of Athens had money to spend on statues, paintings, and beautiful buildings. They had time to read and write and discuss ideas. This was a time of great achievement in Greece — the Classical period.

The Peloponnesian War

Pericles' great achievement was to inspire the artists of Athens to create beautiful work. He wanted everyone to see the glory of Athens. He also wanted Athens to be powerful. Many Athenians dreamed of the day when Greece would become one state with Athens as the capital. The Athenian navy began to attack some city-states and force them to join the Athenian empire.

Sparta had never joined the Delian League because the Spartans did not agree with Athenian ideas. The smaller city-states asked Sparta to help them put an end to the wealth and power of Athens. Sparta joined with supporters in the south to form the

▽ This map shows how power was divided in the war. Sparta controlled the area called the Peloponnese in the south. Athens had supporters on the islands and in western Asia.

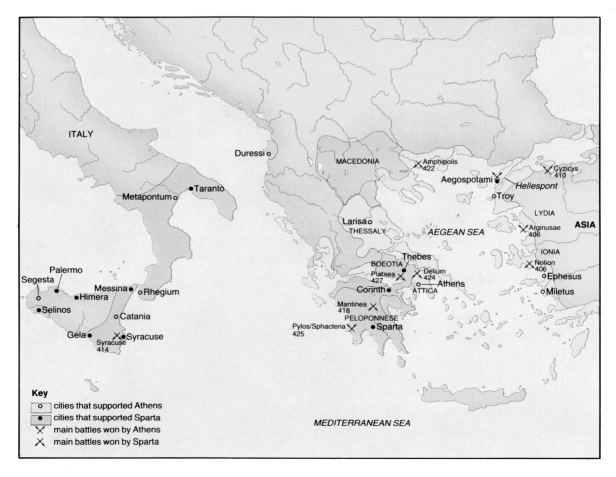

ITALY

Duressi o

MACEDONIA

Amphipolis ✕ 422

Cyzicys ✕ 410

Aegospotami ●

Hellespont

Taranto ●

Metapontum o

Troy o

LYDIA

Larisa o
THESSALY

AEGEAN SEA

Arginusae ✕ 406

ASIA

IONIA

Notion ✕ 406

Thebes ●

BOEOTIA

Ephesus o

Palermo ●

Segesta o

Messina ● o Rhegium

Himera ●

Plataea ● ✕ Delium ✕ 424
427

Athens o

ATTICA

Miletus o

Corinth ●

Selinos ●

Mantinea ✕ 418

o Catania

PELOPONNESE

Gela ● ✕ ● Syracuse

Syracuse 414

Pylos/Sphacteria ✕ 425

Sparta ●

Key

o	cities that supported Athens
●	cities that supported Sparta
✕	main battles won by Athens
✕	main battles won by Sparta

MEDITERRANEAN SEA

Lysander and Alcibiades

Two names appear in writings about the Peloponnesian War. Plato writes of Alcibiades, who was an Athenian. He wanted to be rich and famous and he hoped that the war would bring him power. It was his idea to attack Sicily, and this brought about the first downfall of the Athenian fleet. The fleet was finally defeated by a grim and cunning Spartan, the admiral Lysander, in 405 B.C.

△ The historian Thucydides fought in the Peloponnesian War and felt bitter because Athens was taken over by Sparta. He wrote a detailed account of the war which is our main source of evidence. This bust of Thucydides was made many years after his death but people think this is what he really looked like.

Peloponnesian League. They declared war on the Athenians in 431 B.C.

The Peloponnesian War lasted for 27 years. Farms near Athens were ruined by constant fighting but the Spartans could not capture Athens. They could not storm the strong city walls which linked the city with the harbor at Piraeus. The Athenian navy attacked Sparta's supporters from the sea. Corinth had a trading navy but the Peloponnesian League did not have enough ships to defeat Athens at sea.

The battles went on until the Spartans agreed to accept help from the Persians. This gave them enough money to build a fleet. A Spartan general, Lysander, finally defeated the Athenian fleet by a surprise attack in the harbor at Aegospotami on the Hellespont.

Then Lysander sailed back to Piraeus. His ships stopped food from getting to Athens. Starvation forced the city to surrender in 404 B.C.

Aristophanes' play *Lysistrata* is about the Peloponnesian War. He shows that women wanted to end the wars. Many soldiers were killed and the women were left alone. "Our only armor is our perfume, our dresses, our pretty little shoes," they say in Aristophanes' play.

△ A Greek woman says a sad farewell to her husband before he goes off to war.

The defeat of the city-states

The defeat of the Athenians by the Spartans brought changes to the city-states. The Spartans were harsh rulers who did not believe in democracy. So although the city-states were pleased to be freed from the powerful rule of the Athenian empire, they soon realized they were in a worse situation than before. The Spartans tried to rule the city-states themselves. Fighting broke out and in 371 B.C. the powerful Spartan army was beaten by a smaller army for the first time.

▽ Philip moved the capital of Macedonia to Pella. He became rich by taking over the gold and silver mines of his neighbors. He trained his men to be fierce soldiers and horsemen. Horses were expensive to feed, so cavalry soldiers were not common in the Greek city-states. This gave Philip an advantage.

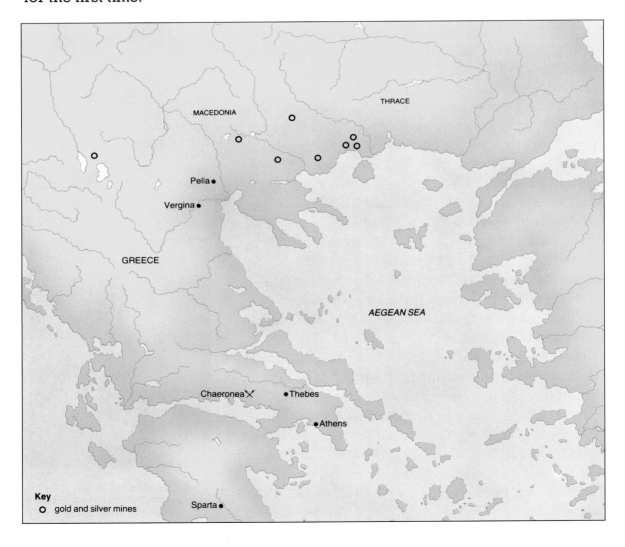

General Epaminondas, from the city-state of Thebes, used a new idea. He formed his Theban soldiers into a crescent shape. When the Spartan army attacked, the Theban soldiers surrounded them. The Thebans put an end to Spartan rule.

Philip of Macedon

Macedonia was a wild mountainous area on the northern borders of Greece. The Macedonians did not all speak Greek. Their way of life was quite different from the city-states. They were ruled by a king. Philip II became king of Macedonia in 359 B.C. He wanted to unite all the city-states of Greece under his rule and then seize lands from Persia. In 338 B.C. Philip's huge army defeated the Greeks at a place called Chaeronea. The Greeks had to accept Philip as their leader. This was the end of democracy in Athens, but the city was still the center of Greek **culture.** This was the age of the great philosophers. The works of Plato, Aristotle, and Xenophanes tell us what the Greeks thought and talked about during this time.

△ This ivory head was found when archaeologists discovered the Macedonians' royal tombs in Vergina in northern Greece. It may represent Philip II.

◁ The tomb at Vergina was full of rich treasures. The tomb contained a golden crown, the gold arrow quiver on the left of the picture, silver bowls and cups, and bronze armor. Writers who knew Philip say that he limped from a war wound. The pair of bronze greaves, to the right and center in this picture, were found in the tomb. One greave was shorter than the other, so archaeologists think they probably belonged to Philip. The tomb itself is decorated with pictures of a lion hunt and there are other fine paintings.

Alexander the Great

When Philip was killed, Alexander said, "Nothing has changed — except the name of the king." Alexander was a brave and brilliant leader who had the same aims as his father. He had been taught by Aristotle, who gave Alexander a love of Greek poetry and art and an interest in science. But, his main interest was in conquering other lands.

First of all, Alexander finally united the old city-states of Greece. Then he was ready to take revenge on Greece's old enemy, Persia. In 334 B.C. he marched into Asia. He defeated the king of Persia, Darius III, and brought all the lands of the Persian empire under Greek rule.

Alexander ruled over Greece, Persia, and Egypt but he realized that people could revolt at any time and destroy his empire. To prevent this, he created Greek colonies in the conquered lands. The colonies were run by his own soldiers. Sixteen of the new colonies were called Alexandria. The city of Alexandria in Egypt became the center of the Greek-speaking world.

Alexander treated the Persians carefully because they had once been the rulers of his empire. He suggested that his men should marry Persian women. He said they should think of all the world as home and all men as their brothers. The Greek soldiers did not like the idea. After all, the Persians had been their enemies for hundreds of years. So Alexander himself married a Persian woman, Roxane from Sogdiana.

After Alexander and his army had been on the march for 10 years, they reached India. Alexander wanted to cross this land which he believed marked the edge of the world. His soldiers, who had been away from their homes and families for a long time, wanted to return. On the way back Alexander caught a fever and died in Babylon in 323 B.C.

Alexander was only 32 when he died. He had made

△ This cameo of Alexander and his Persian wife, Roxane, is carved in onyx. Alexander and Roxane had a young son. Roxane and her son were killed after Alexander's death. As he lay dying, he was asked who should rule after him. He whispered, "The best." No one could agree who the best was. His generals fought over the lands, and finally three generals divided the lands among them.

△ Alexander's influence spread far and wide through his empire and lasted long after his death. This elaborate temple was cut into sandstone at Petra, which is in Jordan. The Greek style of columns and decorations is shown here.

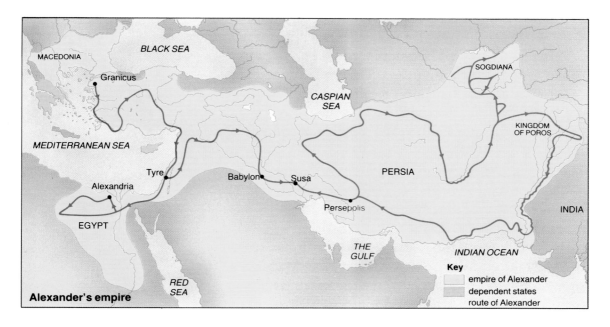

MACEDONIA

BLACK SEA

SOGDIANA

Granicus

CASPIAN
SEA

KINGDOM
OF POROS

MEDITERRANEAN SEA

Tyre

Babylon

Susa

PERSIA

Alexandria

Persepolis

INDIA

EGYPT

THE
GULF

INDIAN OCEAN

Key

empire of Alexander
dependent states
route of Alexander

RED
SEA

Alexander's empire

no plans for his empire after his death. Eventually three of his generals took parts of the empire as kingdoms. Antigonus ruled Macedonia. Seleucus became king of most of Persia. Ptolemy took Egypt. Hellenistic culture and the Greek language dominated these lands for 300 years.

Science in the Hellenistic period

The Hellenistic period was famous for discoveries in science. Alexandria in Egypt was the main center. Ptolemy I set up an institute for research called the Mouseion, or museum and library, next to his palace. It was a place where poets, scientists, and scholars could study. There the mathematicians Euclid and Archimedes worked out rules in geometry. Scholars studied medicine, machines, and the stars. The astronomer Aristarchus learned that the sun, and not the earth, is the center of our universe. Eratosthenes worked out the distance around the earth, and he was very nearly correct. He saw that the sun at Assuan, in the south, was directly overhead, or vertical, in midsummer. He then measured the shadow of a vertical pole at Alexandria in midsummer. He made his calculations from this angle.

△ Alexander fought for 11 years to form his empire. He set out with an army of 30,000 foot soldiers and 5,000 cavalry. They were Greeks and Macedonians. In 334 B.C. he defeated a Persian army at the Granicus River. Then he carried on south to defeat Tyre and Egypt. In 331 he captured the winter palace of the Persian kings at Babylon and went on to take their summer palace at Susa and the ceremonial palace at Persepolis. He spent three years defeating the eastern part of the Persian empire and marched into India. He then defeated the Indian King Poros in 326 B.C. Alexander's horse Bucephalus died in the battle. Alexander wanted to go on to the Ganges River but his tired soldiers refused. Alexander agreed to turn back.

The rise of Rome

T he Romans had built a trading center on the Tiber River in southern Italy. This later became the city of Rome. The Romans began to trade with the cities around the Mediterranean Sea. They were greedy for power. By 201 B.C. they had conquered the wealthy city of Carthage in North Africa and the island of Sicily and country of Spain were under its control. Then they turned their attention to Greece. Mainland Greece was soon under Roman rule. The Greek historian Polybius was taken to Rome as a captive by Aemilius Paullus. He wrote a *World History* to explain the rise of Rome to Greek readers.

The kingdoms in the eastern Mediterranean were gradually taken over by Rome. First of all Macedonia was weakened by fighting with Greeks from the south. Then in 168 B.C. the kingdom was destroyed by a Roman army. The Roman general Pompey defeated the last Seleucid king of Syria in 65 B.C. Cleopatra was the last of the Ptolemies in Egypt. The Roman ruler Octavian took Egypt in 30 B.C., and Cleopatra killed herself. The Romans had become powerful rulers.

◁ The Renaissance began as a study of Classical Greece but artists soon took on a style of their own. They were inspired by the work of the ancient Greeks but they did not copy them. The "School of Athens" shows how the Renaissance painter Raphael imagined the philosophers of ancient Greece.

The legacy of Greece

The Romans were fascinated by Greek culture. As Homer had written about earlier invaders, "Captive Greece made captive her rude conqueror." They took Greek works of art to Rome and copied Greek styles of architecture. Young Romans went to Athens to learn from the philosophers and artists. Greek literature was copied by scholars and taken to Rome.

Rome was conquered by invaders in A.D. 476. Philosophy, art, and literature were almost forgotten in western Europe for nearly 1,000 years. Then, during the 14th century, scholars in Italy began to study Greek so that they could read Greek literature and philosophy. Painters and sculptors were again inspired by the art of Classical Greece. Wealthy Italians paid archaeologists to look for Greek statues. This was the start of the **Renaissance,** or rebirth of thought and art. The civilization of ancient Greece has influenced people ever since.

△ This pot was made at the factory of the English potter, Josiah Wedgwood, in about 1790. You can see that it is similar in style to the pots of ancient Greece but it is more elegant and delicate. The work of the Greeks still inspires artists and craftsmen to use their talents and create beautiful, original designs after thousands of years.

◁ The British Museum in London, England, was built in 1915. It has Ionic columns and carved decorations that are similar to those of ancient Greece. They show how the Greek style has influenced architects all over the world.

Time line

B.C.

c 3000 First Greek-speaking peoples invade Greek mainland.
Minoan civilization begins on Crete.

1600 Mycenaean civilization of Greece begins. Small, rich kingdoms flourish.

1200 The kingdoms of the Mycenaeans are threatened by the Dorians from the north.

1150 The Mycenaean kingdoms are destroyed. The Mycenaean age ends and the Dark Ages begin.

850 – 600 Homer writes his epic poems, the *Iliad* and the *Odyssey*.
The Greeks adopt a new alphabet. Some people begin to leave their Greek homeland and set up colonies in the land around the Mediterranean Sea.
The Dark Ages end and the Archaic period begins.

776 First Olympic Games held.

600 – 500 During the Archaic period many city-states are governed by oligarchies.
The first Greek coins are made. By the end of this period democracy begins in Athens.

546 The Persians conquer Ionia as their empire spreads.

500 Archaic period ends.
Classical period begins.

493 Ionian and Athenian supporters try to rebel against Persian rule, but are defeated.

490 Persians invade Greece and raid Athens. They are defeated at the Battle of Marathon.

480 Persian fleet defeated by Athenians at the Battle of Salamis.

479 Greeks defeat Persian armies at Plataea.
End of Persian invasions.

477 Delian League set up between Athens and other Greek city-states.

449 Peace made with Persia.
Athens begins to flourish under its new leader, Pericles, and the Parthenon is built.

431 – 404 The Peloponnesian War is fought between Athens and Sparta.

404 Athens surrenders to Sparta. The Spartan empire is created but the Spartans have difficulty controlling it.

371 Spartans defeated by Theban general, Epaminondas, at the Battle of Leuctra. Sparta's power is broken forever.

356 Philip II becomes king of Macedonia and his son Alexander the Great is born.

c 350   Philip tries to take over the city-states.

338   Philip defeats Athenian League at Battle of Chaeronea and dominates Greece.

336   Philip murdered. Alexander becomes king of Macedonia.

334 – 323 Alexander founds his empire, invading and defeating the Persian empire.

323   Alexander dies at Babylon and his huge empire is split by his generals. Ptolemy takes Egypt and Seleucus takes Persia. The Classical period ends and the Hellenistic period begins.

200   The age of Greek scientific discovery follows, based around Alexandria in Egypt.

100   Rome gains power in Asia Minor, as the Greek civilization declines.

30   Cleopatra, the last ruler of Ptolemy's family, loses her Egyptian kingdom to Rome.

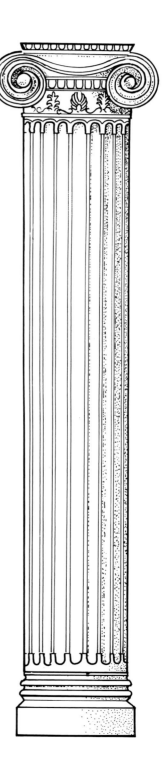

Glossary

abacus: a frame with rows of sliding beads on wires or in grooves, which is used for counting

administration: the management or organization of something

amphidromia: a ceremony at which a baby is named. Today, we call this the "christening"

apprentice: someone who works for a skilled person in return for being taught that skill

archaeologist: a person who finds out about the past by studying old buildings and objects

aristocracy: a country, or part of a country, that is ruled by a small group of its richest and most powerful people

aulos: a V-shaped Greek musical instrument made of two pipes that were both blown into at once. One was then played with the right hand and one with the left

cavalry: soldiers on horseback who fought outside the group of foot soldiers

ceremony: a formal ritual or occasion. The parts of a ceremony usually follow a strict pattern or order

chiton: a simple tunic or robe made from two lengths of cloth fastened together at the shoulders and belted at the waist

citizen: any member of a country, or part of a country, who is allowed to take part in choosing its rulers

city-state: part of a country that includes the city at its center and the countryside around it. Each city-state had its own ruler

civilization: to live according to a series of rules and laws. Civilizations are made up of groups of people who live together and obey the same rules

colony: a group of people who settle away from their own country, but still consider themselves to be part of it

cosmetics: substances used on the skin, especially the face, that are intended to improve a person's appearance. Today, we usually call this "makeup"

culture: the ways in which a civilization improves itself and develops. Different countries grow up in different ways, so they all have different cultures

democracy: a country or part of a country that is ruled by a group of people chosen by all its citizens

fortify: to make stronger. A fortified town is one protected by a strong wall that is built around it

foundation: the base on which a building stands. Foundations, usually built under the ground, are needed to support a building properly

herbalism: the study and use of herbs for treating illness

himation: a cloak worn by the women of ancient Greece over a tunic. The himation was usually made of wool

Hippocratic oath: the oath, or promise, created by Hippocrates, as a code of correct behavior for people who treat the sick. Doctors still have to take this oath today before they can practice medicine

interest: extra money charged by a bank or moneylender on top of the amount loaned. The interest is a payment for the use of the bank's money

invest: to put money into something. Investors hope to make more money from their investment

league: a group of people or countries who share the same beliefs and have the same aims

linen: a type of cloth made from the woven fibers of the flax plant

mosaic: a design or picture made of small pieces of colored stone or glass

myth: a legend, or traditional story, that is based on fantasy rather than fact

obol: a silver coin of ancient Greece

oligarchy: a country, or part of a country, that is governed by only a few of its people

oracle: a place where people could consult the gods, usually through a special priest or priestess who might also be known as the oracle

peltasts: lightly armed soldiers who fought on either side of the main body of soldiers in battle

phalanx: the formation in which the hoplites, or foot soldiers, fought in battle

philosopher: someone who seeks the truth, a thinker

Renaissance: a new beginning. A period beginning in the fourteenth century when the European people emerged from their Dark Ages and began to study the art and thinking of Classical Greece

sanctuary: a holy place. Churches and temples are sanctuaries

sculpture: a work of art that is carved or molded, rather than painted. Statues are sculptures

surgery: cutting into part of a person's body to treat or remove something

symposium: a drinking party and talk held after a feast. Symposiums were often accompanied by musical entertainment

tenant farmer: a farmer who does not own the land he works. He may rent it or be employed by the owner

terrace: a flat area which is not level with the ground. Vines are often grown on a series of terraces cut into a hillside like large, shallow steps

threshold: a point of entry to a building. The threshold is usually a plank or stone at the bottom of the door into a house

trireme: a Greek warship with sails and three rows of oars, one above the other

yarn: long spun thread that is prepared for weaving, knitting, or sewing

Index